TIMELESS PLACES

VENICE

ALEXANDRA BONFANTE-WARREN

FRIEDMAN/FAIRFAX
PUBLISHERS

A FRIEDMAN/FAIRFAX BOOK
Friedman/Fairfax Publishers
15 West 26 Street
New York, NY 10010
Telephone (212) 685-6610
Fax (212) 685-1307
Please visit our website: www.metrobooks.com

Library of Congress Cataloging-in-Publication Data.

Bonfante-Warren, Alexandra.
    Venice / Alexandra Bonfante-Warren
        p. cm. — (Timeless Places)
    Includes index.
    ISBN 1-56799-788-0
    1. Venice (Italy)—Pictoral works.   2. Venice (Italy)—History.   I. Series.

DG674.7 .B67 2000
945'.31—dc21   99-056401

Editors: Nathaniel Marunas and Ann Kirby
Art Director: Jeff Batzli
Designer: John Marius
Photography Editor: Wendy Missan
Production: Richela Fabian and Camille Lee

Color separations by Spectrum Pte Ltd
Printed in Hong Kong by Midas Printing Limited

1 3 5 7 9 10 8 6 4 2

Distributed by Sterling Publishing Co., Inc.
387 Park Avenue South
New York, NY 10016-8810
Orders and customer service (800) 367-9692
Fax: (800) 542-7567
E-mail: *custservice@sterlingpub.com*
Website: *www.sterlingpublishing.com*

❧

PAGE 1: **Venice is a modern metropolis that guards its ancient secrets.**

The narrow *rii* in dim, perpetual shadows recall that all cities have private histories.

PAGES 2–3: **One of the jewels of Venice, the palazzo Contarini-Dal Zaffo was built at the turn of the sixteenth century with a vast garden alongside.**

Beside it, the sober palazzo Brandolin-Rota was home to the English poets Robert Browning and Elizabeth Barrett Browning.

CONTENTS

PAGES 4–5: **For centuries, this sight greeted the returning mariners and merchants of Venice. The Republic's ships were laden with the scent of spices and the billows of silk—all the fabulous goods of the eastern trade routes.**

PAGE 6: **Private homes and gardens seem to float along side the placid waters of the Canal Grande. The tranquility of the surrounding lagoon earned Venice its reputation as** *la Serrenissima.*

RIGHT: **A flooded piazza San Marco looks dreamlike, but the danger that the** *acqua alta* **poses to the city is all too real.**

PART 1

STORIA

A MEMORY OF A DREAM OVER WATER, VENICE RISES FROM ITS OWN REFLECTIONS, A SHIMMERING, ELUSIVE HARMONY OF CONTRASTS, OF GOLD, GLASS, AND STONE AS DELICATE AND ARTFULLY WROUGHT AS LACE, THE LAST ERODING REMNANT OF A GORGEOUS REPUBLIC, GENTLY SUBSIDING INTO THE SEA AND CENTURIES OF DEMOCRACY. EVERYONE HAS AN IDEA OF VENICE: GONDOLAS, CANALS, CARNIVAL, MASS TOURISM, OR JUST SITTING AT HARRY'S BAR SIPPING BELLINIS—THOSE INIMITABLE LATE-SUMMER MARRIAGES OF FRESH PEACH JUICE AND PROSECCO, THE SPARKLING WHITE WINE OF THE VENETO. LIKEWISE, EVERYONE HAS A CONNECTION TO VENICE: *THE MERCHANT OF . . .* ; *DEATH IN . . .* ; GIORGIONE'S PUZZLES; THE FLESHY BOUDOIRS OF TITIAN AND TINTORETTO IN RICHER-THAN-REAL COLOR; GUARDI'S AND CANALETTO'S MISTY WATERSCAPES; TURNER'S EXPLOSIVE LIGHTSCAPES; CASANOVA'S DARING ESCAPE FROM THE GRIM EMBRACE OF THE PIOMBI PRISONS; OR THE STRAINS OF VIVALDI'S FURIOUSLY ELEGANT *SEASONS*.

WOVEN INTO THE COLOR AND UNMISTAKABLE LIGHT OF ITS ART AND ITS MUSIC, THE HANDSOME, FEMININE SPLENDOR OF ITS BUILDINGS, IS VENICE'S ETERNAL AWARENESS OF THE DUALITY OF LIFE AND DEATH. THIS CONSCIOUSNESS DRAWS ITS INSPIRATION FROM THE LAGOON, A VAST EXPANSE COVERING NEARLY 215 SQUARE MILES (550 KM²). ALMOST EXACTLY HALF IS NORMALLY COVERED WITH WATER, AND THIS IS CALLED THE *LAGUNA VIVA*—THE LIVING LAGOON, DOTTED WITH THE ANCIENT ISLETS OF THIS ETERNAL SITE. THE OTHER HALF IS ONLY SOMETIMES FLOODED, AND THIS IS THE *LAGUNA MORTA*—THE DEAD LAGOON, A PLACE SO RICH IN WILDLIFE THAT THE QUALIFIER "DEAD" SEEMS HARDLY TO APPLY.

❧

PAGES 10–11: **The Arsenale, which sent Venetian ships throughout the Mediterranean, also produced cannons and other weapons. It was under constant construction or restoration from the twelfth century, as tradition has it, until the nineteenth. The two towers were originally built in 1574.**

OPPOSITE: **More than most cities, Venice has public and private faces. While the *porta* on the canal is both practical and formal, in the back, every palazzo has doors opening onto tiny, winding *calli*. This is a place where the fantastic and the everyday are intimately entwined.**

Surveying this magical city, whether from atop a column in the piazzetta or from wellheads and portals throughout the city, is the winged lion of the Apocrypha, the mystical emblem of Saint Mark the Evangelist. This fabulous beast, a trophy brought back from the East, is the proud symbol of the trade routes that for a thousand years poured wealth into the Republic of San Marco.

La serenissima repubblica di Venezia—the Most Serene Republic of Venice. Some say this title comes from the stillness of the mirroring lagoon, but in the city's heyday the canal and lagoon were anything but tranquil, their waters cleaved by ships from every port in the Mediterranean, their docks alive with the colors, costumes, customs, and gestures of a thousand places. And the Republic's history is anything but unembattled, even today. Venice shared in all the vicissitudes of its times: famines, plagues, fires, floods. No, the Republic was and is serene just as majesty is serene. It is sublime and august, a place with eternity's gaze, a vision of power before and beyond arrogance, as hieratic as the Byzantine saints that watch from the gilded mosaics of San Marco.

Venice is famous for two things: for being beautiful and for being impossible; it is impossibly beautiful. Against all odds, the city seems to survive time and tide; it should long ago have collapsed into the lagoon, its foundations eroded by the ceaselessly lapping tides. It is only appropriate that the city's opera house, La Fenice (The Phoenix), conjures up the mythical bird that rises from its own ashes—the theater itself was just rebuilt after a fire in 1996.

Appearances, and the myth of Venice, are deceiving. The city that has withstood natural, political, and military disaster is more threatened than ever. The rivers that once brought timber down from the northern forests now wash agricultural poisons into the lagoon and canals. Industrial pollution from Marghera and Mestre attacks the Istrian stone of which much of the city is made. However, efforts have been made to protect the city. For example, the industrial development of northeastern Italy severely depleted the water table, weakening the very ground Venice rests upon and causing the islands to sink measurably. In the mid-1970s the government limited the drawing of water from the city's underground wells, which allowed the water pressure to build up again and the subsidence to stop. And the magistrates of La Serenissima have been able to direct the channeling of the river waters, which to some extent mitigated the power of the

❧

The lion of the evangelist Saint Mark holds an open book, symbolizing the spread of the Christian Gospel. The ancient proud symbol of La Serenissima reigns lordly from the tympan of Saint Mark's Basilica.

tides; in 1988 a system of barriers was put in place at the Lido to help manage the periodic flooding that threatens the city. The preservation of Venice has become an international affair, supported not only by individuals and groups, but by UNESCO, the United Nations Educational, Scientific, and Cultural Organization.

Everyone's ideas of Venice are true, but put them all together and this city in the lagoon, with its 118 islands and four hundred bridges, will still elude definition. It is the city of water above all others: of rivers pouring into the lagoon and the Adriatic Sea, but also of the hundreds of *rii* threading their way between the hundred islets. It was these waters that largely made the city's wealth possible, providing the rinsing required by the textile dyers and cleansing Venice with the power and rhythm of the tides.

The historical center occupies some six square miles (15 km²) distributed on either side of the Canal Grande, from the *sestiere*, or "sixth," of Cannaregio in the northwest, to San Polo, Santa Croce, and Dorsoduro west of the canal, and San Marco and Castello to the east. Then there is the lagoon and its islands: Giudecca, still nearly as quiet as when Michelangelo praised its tranquility; the Isola di San Giorgio Maggiore; the cemetery island of San Michele; Torcello, the former heart of the Republic; Burano, famous for its lacemakers; and Murano, known for its glassmakers. The beach island, the Lido, with its once-fashionable turn-of-the-century villas, plush grand hotels, and modern architecture, has again become one of Europe's most popular resorts.

Venice is home to some 340,000 people; of these, only about 100,000 live in the historic center, the *sestieri*, where rents are inflated, buildings tend to be damp, and modern amenities, from parks to supermarkets, can be few. Many have moved to the modern areas of Mestre and Marghera, following the jobs. Almost half the homes in Venice are uninhabited, the property of outsiders who alight only once or twice a year.

Yet Venice is a living, lively city, where it seems that everyone knows everyone else, and neighbors always have time to

A wealthy merchant unloaded goods from all over the Mediterranean and beyond onto the ground floor of this canalside palazzo. Upstairs, the family found refuge from the summer's heat in the loggia.

stop and exchange a few words. It has been a long time since Venice was threatened by outsiders, and the city has little history of defensive battles. Today's "invaders" swarm piazza San Marco (called simply "la piazza" by the Venetians), the Rialto, and the shops of the Mercerie, but for the most part, the farther recesses of Venice remain private. Shopkeepers mind the store, artisans tend to their craft, the fishermen go out with their nets, and the shipbuilders construct and repair boats, both working and ceremonial. Venice has no end of boats; the fishing, hunting, and racing craft glide down the city's waterways, their names and variety echoing down the years.

Boats are an integral part of life in Venice: not only the gondola, but the *sandalo, mascareta,* and *cofano, the sciopon, caorlina, sampierota,* and *topo*—the latter meaning, simply, "mouse." Even ordinary city services—sanitation, ambulances, fire fighters, and police—are handled by boat. True to a thousand-year tradition, produce is shipped by boat to the Rialto, and from there to markets throughout the city. In the off-season, or in areas of the city less frequented by tourists, there is an elusive charm, the reason for which comes as a pleasing realization: Venice moves *a passo d'uomo,* at human pace. In the canals, the ferries—whose advent in 1881 dealt the deathblow to the gondolas—chug from stop to stop, while occasional motorboats roar by. The city's few remaining gondolas glide silently down the rii, as planes roar overhead to and from nearby Marco Polo International Airport.

Tourism, of course, is a major industry, and tourists make up many of the fifty thousand or so people who pour into Venice from the mainland each day. Almost one third of those employed in the city work in tourism, now a year-round industry. Most of Venice's "industries" are small, specialized shops that turn out some of the finest objects in the world. The jewelry shops displaying unique high-end pieces continue the active trade that has characterized these shores since before Roman

Every visitor to Venice experiences a moment of enchantment. For some, it happens at dusk, when the water and sky glimmer like silk with tints of violet, blue, and gold.

times. Even the decorative paper available at every souvenir stand harks back more than five hundred years, to the days of a Venice-based French printer, Nicolas Jensen—the first to use Roman, rather than Gothic, type.

The Venetian tradition of papermaking, like so much of the city's history, is tied to the city's greatness as an exporter of textiles. When fabrics, infinitely reused and transformed, could no longer be salvaged even to be sold to the poorest of the poor, the rags were used to make paper. La Serenissima manufactured the highest-quality, and costliest, fabrics in Europe. In the mercantile era, beginning in the thirteenth century, the master weavers and dyers jealously guarded their professional secrets, protecting their city's reputation for inimitable shades. The unmatchable brilliance of Venetian red, for example, was attributed to the specific saline content of the canals in which the fabrics were rinsed, but the masters of the dyeworks also spread tales of demons lurking in the neighborhood, to discourage industrial spies.

Perhaps the most uniquely Venetian crafts are those related to Carnival, the Catholic world's farewell to revelry as it moves into Lent. The most celebrated of these artifacts are the *baute*, the Carnival masks, and the tricorns completing the extravagant costumes that turn the late-winter week before Ash Wednesday into a phantasmagorical, mysteriously erotic shimmer of priceless silks, lace, gold, and silver, swirling in the private ballrooms of the palazzi. Luxury fabrics are still made in Venice, but the hand looms are few now, replaced by machines that can weave far more than the sixteen inches a day (41cm) that the hand looms could produce.

Three sites most visibly stand for Venice's mystical convergence of powers: the Rialto Bridge, representing the city's commercial life force; Piazza San Marco, joining heavenly and ducal power; and the Arsenale, the heart of the Venetian empire's naval prowess, both mercantile and military.

The Rialto, in the sestiere di San Polo, is traditionally considered the first center of Venice, where the young Republic

❦

Today, glass is Venice's most famous product, but color is the secret of its history. For a few thousand *lire*,
a traveler can take home a strand of glamour, a necklace of light.

moved in the eleventh century after leaving the islands of the lagoon. The first bridge to span the Canal Grande, the Rialto is still surrounded today by busy shops and markets, telling the tale of early medieval society in the names of the streets around it, such as ruga degli Orefici, which housed the goldsmiths' shops, ruga degli Speziali, home to the spice merchants, and La Pescheria, which held the fishmongers' stalls.

However rigidly compartmentalized Venetian society was, in the heyday of the Republic's commercial glory it did allow the wealth to trickle down to some degree. Those outside this sea- and warfaring economy tended to be women: the orphaned, widowed, and abandoned, the sisters of sailors lost at sea, the mothers of soldiers killed in battle, the wives of wanderers who simply stayed put in some foreign port. However invisible as the poorest of the poor, women were more prominent in Venice than in other European cities, as is evident in the architectural legacy of the numerous convents, hospices, and schools built to save, shelter, and train them.

In the thirteenth and fourteenth centuries, as its wealth multiplied, the city built social service institutions, such as hospices for the indigent and old, alongside those of the religious orders. But these were also the first years of the great palazzi on the Canal Grande, today some of the world's most discreetly magnificent hotels: the Danieli, Gritti, and, on Giudecca, Cipriani. In the more modest neighborhoods, the hunger for living space produced the so-called barbicans, extensions built out from the second stories and above, between which Venice's brilliant blue sky appears as scant celestial strips.

In the Baroque era of the seventeenth century, when appearances were an integral element of power, certain areas of the city began to resemble the wings of a theater: the mazelike, moss-grown alleys winding away behind the airy Byzantine, Gothic, Renaissance, or Baroque façades facing each other across the Canal Grande in a dazzling, courtly dance.

The unparalleled prosperity of the Venetians derived from a singularly adroit merging of diplomacy, warfare, and timing—the secret of political and financial success. The history of the Republic is a ceaseless balancing act, a continuous search for the equilibrium of power that would best serve the Republic as a whole, more than any single group—despite the patricians' traditional domination of the rosters of doges, Senate, and magistracies. At the same time, Venice asserted its power abroad, deploying with knowing, even cynical, theatricality the diplomatic effect of opulent elegance, as in Palazzo Venezia, the Republic's former embassy in Rome. Its policies must have worked: the city has had no defensive walls around it since the twelfth century.

For all its military involvement in wars local and distant, Venice remained essentially neutral, forging diplomatic alliances that served its commercial interests above all, even during the bloody wars between the supporters of the pope and those of the Holy Roman Emporer. This avoidance of conflict also characterizes the Venetian dialect: no hard consonants halt the tongue; instead, sounds dissolve into soft sibilants. Even identity blurs: the church of San Zanipolo celebrates no obscure single saint, but two of the apostles, *Giovanni e Paolo*, John and Paul. Inside, the church honors the unity of Venetian church and state: everywhere, tombs of the doges and their wives, the *dogorosso*, boast the names that resound through the history of the Republic of San Marco: Alvise Mocenigo and Loredana Marcello; Silvestro Valier and Elisabetta Querini Valier; and many others, their monuments and surroundings created by the greatest artists of their world and their day.

Many of the palazzi once inhabited by the city's patricians and merchants now house museums and other cultural institutions, their stuccoed *salotti*

ringing with elegant fundraising events that bring together the world's elite. But the old aristocratic families survive, too, tapped into the international commerce of the new millennium, and in the winter time at Carnival, gondolas glide up to the elaborate canalside water doors, and silk-clad ladies and gentlemen step, like gleaming ghosts, from the narrow boats into the palazzi, entering candlelit ballrooms—living silhouettes of a past inextricably wed to the present.

Il Dogado

To modern eyes, Venice can look like a pale, pretty, and tremulous survivor—which it is—but its very longevity adds a subtle strength to its identity. The region of Venice, known as the Veneto, has been inhabited since prehistoric times, when at least some of its people arrived by ship from the eastern Mediterranean. The earliest traces of habitation go back to the late Bronze Age, from the eleventh to the ninth century B.C.E., revealing organized agriculture and animal husbandry.

A thousand years later, the Veneti, like so many of the Italic peoples, were gradually absorbed into the expanding Roman empire—the emperor Augustus, in his reorganization of the Italian peninsula around the first century C.E., recognized their distinctive culture when he named the region Venetia. Tradition (or legend) traces the genealogy of the Veneti to the Trojans, following their defeat by the Greeks. The first classical historians commented on the landscape of the lagoons,

La Sensa, as the Venetians call the midsummer feast of the Ascension, brings out brightly hued and gorgeously decorated longboats, in memory of the pomp of the Doge's Marriage of Venice with the Sea.

which have long been lively, profitable, and, for the most part, healthy, unlike the malarial stretches on the western coast of the Italian peninsula. Washed by numerous rivers that deposited fertile soil, the prosperous early cities on the Adriatic coast traded objects and local salt with the cities of mainland Italy, as well as with the far reaches of the Aegean and beyond.

As the Western Roman Empire eroded, it could no longer protect its population from the northern barbarians. West of the Appenines, the people of the towns, repeatedly beset by invaders, ultimately dispersed into the countryside. In the northeast, they moved onto some sixty islands in the lagoon for safety. There, the Venetians flourished thanks to the abundance of fish and marsh

fowl, and their monopoly on salt. Torcello, today a remote hinterland dotted with imposing monuments from the city's earliest Christian era, was the lagoon's most important island from the fifth to the tenth century.

It was on Torcello in 697 that Venice elected its first doge—from the Latin *dux*, meaning "leader" or "general." The expansion of the Eastern Roman Empire eventually embraced the duchy of Venice, which remained a vassal of the empire until the tenth century. This relationship with the Byzantine splendor of Constantinople, and by extension with the Silk Road of Asia, would continue for centuries, through fierce wars, pragmatic alliances, and bloody betrayals.

Emblematic of the importance of the new state was the assignment in 775 of a bishop to the Venetians. This first prelate, Obelerio, lived on the island then known as *del Castello*. Today a virtually uninhabited fishing community, San Pietro del Castello was the first seat of Venetian religious power, the bishopric until 1451, and the patriarchate until 1807, when San Marco replaced San Pietro as the city's cathedral.

Around 827, Agnello Partecipazio, the reigning doge and first of a dynasty of seven, moved the seat of government to the Rialto. The merchants of Torcello and Malamocco honored him with a relic of the evangelist Mark, smuggled out of Alexandria, it is said, in a load of pork (which the Muslims would have refused to touch, let alone search). The basilica, later cathedral, of San Marco, was begun in 829; it would become a visible record of the transformations of the Republic, acquiring architectural additions and

In the narthex of Saint Mark's Basilica, against a golden sky, a thirteenth-century mosaic shows Saint Mark's church, bronze horses and all, when it was the chapel of the *doges*. King, queen, and courtiers emerge to pay homage to two bishop saints.

ornamentations for the next eight centuries. Also in the first half of the ninth century, the Doges' Palace was built nearby, in the shadow of the saint's protection.

Late in the eleventh century, the seagoing Normans, now masters of southern Italy, attempted to place a stranglehold on trade in the Adriatic. When the Venetians destroyed the Norman blockade, they won the gratitude of the Byzantine Empire—with all the material advantages it implied. Little more than a decade later, with the First Crusade in 1096, it became evident that the Venetians considered these privileges their due. Impelled by a web of motives, this mission to free Jerusalem from the "infidels" would succeed within months, at the cost of tens of thousands of lives on both sides. The economic consequences were dramatic: the ports of southern Europe, in particular Genoa and Pisa, battened on the subsequent Crusades, making fortunes victualling ships and carrying troops to the Levant.

The Venetians, faced with this increasing commercial rivalry, simply went in and destroyed the Genoese and Pisan quarters of Constantinople. The Byzantine emperor John II Comnenus refused to renew the Venetians' commercial privileges, and in the late 1100s a number of Venetian traders found their goods expropriated and themselves in jail. With the uncanny ability to snatch victory from defeat that characterized the great centuries of La Serenissima, the Venetians were soon prospering once more. Nevertheless, the violence suffered at the hands of the Byzantine emperor would not go unavenged: in 1202, during the Fourth Crusade, the great doge Enrico Dandolo, in his eighties and nearly blind, led

the fleet that conquered Constantinople, ravaging the city "with a carnage almost unparalleled in history," as one historian puts it. When the dust settled, the Venetians owned three-eighths of the Byzantine holdings, as well as the Aegean islands of Corfu and Crete.

It was also in the thirteenth century that a Venetian merchant family set out on a voyage that would win them immortality. In 1271, seventeen-year-old Marco Emilione Polo left Venice with his father and uncle on a journey to the Great Khan, with a letter the Mongol leader had requested from the Pope explaining certain points of Christian doctrine. By 1274, the Polos had crossed the Gobi Desert to reach Yunnan, in what is today southern China, but was then occupied by the conqueror Kublai Khan. In 1280, Marco saw the Pacific Ocean, the first European recorded to have done so.

In 1292, Marco left the Khan's service to return home by way of Sumatra, India, and Persia. By then the Crusades were waning, and a new power was emerging in Bithynia, in what is today northwest Turkey: Othman al-Ghazi, chief of the Seljuk Turks, would found the Ottoman Empire, destined to challenge Venetian domination of much of eastern Europe and the Mediterranean for almost four hundred years.

Back in Venice in 1295, Marco found his city mightier than ever. The expansion of the Arsenale, which had been going on for several generations, was continuing. Just as the activities around the Rialto had given their names to the *rughe* and *calli* of that area, so too, around the Arsenale were the calle del Piombo (Lead Street), calle della Pegola (Tar Street), and calle delle Vele (Sail Street).

In 1297, Venice restricted political rights to about twelve hundred patrician families listed in the Golden Book; from among these families were chosen the 480 members of the Maggior Consiglio, or Greater Council, essentially the Republic's parliament. The sharp narrowing of the number of people with access to power naturally provoked unrest; in reaction, the Republic created the Council of Ten, with broad authority and with responsibilities ranging from maintaining the city's infrastructure to protecting its security. With typically Venetian clarity of purpose, this engine of social surveillance not only thwarted nascent popular rebellions, but also ducal attempts at absolute authority: in 1355, the Council condemned the doge Marin Faliero to death for trying to have himself declared prince, inspiring a tragedy by Byron.

It is one of the fundamental paradoxes of the story of Venice that, so long inhabited, it grew so quickly when it did grow: in the twelfth century, the city's only bridge was the wooden drawbridge of Rialto. The groundwork for most of the city was laid over the next two centuries, when Venice would mushroom. The original foundations of most constructions were wood posts pounded into the soft bed of the lagoon; because of the chemical composition of the water, this wood calcified, thus becoming resistant to the pull and push of the tides. On top of the posts was laid a flooring of the distinctive white Istrian stone that helps give the city its luminous, almost lunar fascination. These foundations were extremely costly, so when owners rebuilt they tended to keep them: with all of its later additions, San Marco, like many Venetian churches, still rests on its original Byzantine floor plan. Architectural elements were likewise reused, contributing to Venice's dreamlike quality of overlapping styles.

Thus, in the thirteenth and fourteenth centuries, the city's merchants built houses on the Canal Grande, the case-fondaco, which combined home and warehouse. It was during this period that wooden bridges were replaced with stone or masonry spans, often with steps that horses couldn't climb—with the result that horses were banished from the calli of Venice. The houses along the Canal Grande are the city's history in procession, flaunting a multitude of styles that range from the few remaining case-fondaco to the Oriental lines of the Byzantine, the deceptively pretty Gothic, the aristocratically severe Renaissance, the unexpectedly restrained Baroque, and the ornate Neoclassical.

In order to increase its fleet of warships, in 1325 the Arsenale began an expansion that would not be completed until 1460. The project naturally required many skilled workers, who came to Venice with their families, creating new neighborhoods. Venice became the largest city in Italy, and one of the largest in Europe.

The warships produced by the expanded Arsenale escorted the city's merchant ships as far west as England and up into Flanders, but they also permitted Venice to increase its military presence in the Adriatic and the eastern Mediterranean. During the fourteenth century, Venice would become a true empire, taking cities on the Italian mainland and more territory in the eastern Mediterranean. Meanwhile, the Republic was increasingly embroiled in skirmishes with neighboring Italian and foreign states, not only Genoa, but also France and Hungary.

Venice flourished and was the most sophisticated state in Europe, attracting scholars from throughout the Mediterranean, but when the Black Death struck in the 1340s, it was as helpless as the remotest village. This was far from the first appearance of the bubonic plague, but the extent of the outbreak was unprecedented. After devastating China and the Tatars, Southwest Asia, Egypt, and Asia Minor, the plague raged westward. Originally, port cities like Venice, with its high volume of trade and many rats, carriers of the disease, were the most vulnerable. Estimates of the number of deaths in Venice range from one third of the population to two thirds, but La Serenissima still fared better than those cities that were wiped out by death and by the flight of the living.

When the plague came, many believed the end of the world was upon them. Groups of penitents sprang up, attempt-

ing to atone for the sins of all, sins that must surely have called down this God-sent affliction. A terror nearly as great as the plague itself swept through Europe on its heels: the dread of dying unshriven, that is, without the sacraments. The Avignon pope Clement VI, perhaps out of compassion, perhaps in an attempt to calm the widespread and increasing panic, gave a blanket remission of sin to all those who died of the plague.

The end of the world, however, caused merely intermittent interruptions in the wars of the European world. When Milan annexed Genoa in the 1350s, Venice found itself with a nearby enemy on the mainland. Despite the Visconti threat, in the early 1380s Venice finally defeated Genoa after a closely fought three-year war, waged at Chioggia, the gates of Venice itself, and culminating in a bitter blockade countered by an equally relentless siege of the blockading forces.

The construction of the magnificent Rialto Bridge, which has become one of the emblems of Venice, was assigned to Antonio Da Ponte (whose name means "from the bridge"), who sank six thousand pilons and spent 250,000 ducats to build the elegant span, completed in 1592.

La Dominante

In 1416, the Venetians, under the admiralty of Pietro Loredan, won the first of several battles against the Ottoman Empire; three years later, the Doge's Palace was given a new façade, appropriate to the world power that Venice was becoming. A decade later, the city's position was dominant. Through its characteristic combination of diplomatic finesse and canny military deployment, Venice had established a commercial reign in the Aegean and now ruled important Italian cities of the northeast, including Treviso, Padua, and Verona. In the eastern Mediterranean, however, the Ottomans were becoming unstoppable; despite Venice's adroit maneuver, the Turks took Thessalonica in 1430. When the Ottoman Turks took Constantinople in 1453, toppling the long-lived Eastern Roman Empire, Venice signed a treaty the following year confirming its trading privileges with the new power in the eastern Mediterranean, maintaining its near-monopoly on the spice trade, and merely passing along the higher prices resulting from the Turkish tariffs.

The engineer of many of these negotiations was the doge Francesco Foscari (ruled 1423–57). Under Foscari, Venice once more overcame Milan on the battlefield, winning cities farther inland. In the 1430s, Foscari sent Loredan, now a general, and later a *generalissimo*, back into battle, where he succeeded in reclaiming major possessions along the Po River.

With its territories expanding, Venice was looking more and more to Italy rather than to the Levant, and was soon embroiled in the shifting policies of the mainland. Again, the city's architecture reflected the moment: gone were the functional canalside fondaci and the ornate Byzantine and Gothic façades; in their place rose palazzi in the solemn Florentine Renaissance style.

Despite the treaty of 1454, the Ottomans disrupted Venice's exchanges with the Levant, and in response the Republic attacked Constantinople. The two powers would be at war for sixteen years, with the sultan's forces coming as close as the city's outskirts in 1477. Although Venice ceded some territories, the peace treaty of 1479 restored its trading privileges in the Black Sea—at the cost of a high annual tribute. In 1484, Venice acquired Rovigo, a prosperous agricultural town that would prove to be La Dominante's last territorial expansion. In the years around the turn of the century, Venice serenely withstood several of the incursions that would change the political balance of peninsular Italy, including the invasions of northern Italy by France in 1494, and of southern Italy by Spain in the early sixteenth century. Meanwhile, the Turkish forces were pressing Venice's holdings in the eastern Mediterranean.

The French and Spanish invasions prompted Venice to take action. Mindful, perhaps, of its new vulnerability on land, as well as of the need to extend its agricultural territories in the fertile northern plains, the Republic sought in the early sixteenth century to strengthen its presence on terra firma by invading neighboring Romagna, one of the Papal States. Pope Julius II responded in 1508 by excommunicating the Republic and organizing the League of Cambrai, made up of Spanish, French, and Austrian armies. La Serenissima found itself taking on essentially all of western Europe, pursuing a two-tiered military and diplomatic defense that was not entirely unsuccessful. In an unmatched feat of negotiation, Venice undid the alliance of Cambrai, nation by nation, but forfeited any hopes of further expansion on the Italian mainland. In the end, Julius II, pressed by the Reformation and unwilling to allow armed foreigners to remain in Italy, withdrew the excommunication and reknit an alliance with his sometime adversary. In 1511, the Papal States joined with Venice to chase the French out of northern Italy.

In only a few generations, the economics of the Mediterranean world had changed. Where Venice had held a virtual lock on trade with the east, now Portuguese and Dutch ships were plying the sea route around Africa's Cape of Good Hope to the Indies, and in Christopher Columbus' wake, the Spanish and English were doing a brisk west–east trade. Nevertheless, such were Venice's long-established trade relations with other European nations, the unequalled quality of its manufactured products, and its amassed wealth, that it would continue to sail proudly through another two centuries, defying the decline of its grandeur.

In the sixteenth century, the Republic turned inward: its magistratures addressed a host of public works, from dredging the silted-up waterways to beautifying the city and maintaining the rivers. In town, the palazzi, like the city itself, became increasingly aristocratic in style, while in the country, many patrician families, inspired (in true Renaissance fashion) both by a lofty regard for rural living and by the more pragmatic needs of their newly acquired farmlands, built villas inland.

During this time Venice was increasingly taking on the personality it is known for today, not only visually, in the façades of the palazzi along the Canal Grande, but socially, in its characteristically unique and complex style. Already in the sixteenth century, cosmopolitan Venice had a reputation for sophisticated pleasure;

The architect of Santa Maria della Salute designed the church to look like a crown. Venetian pride of place is never absent: sculptures ride the Baroque volutes of Santa Maria della Salute like waves or like figureheads on a great ship.

emblematic of this reputation were its courtesans. These women, like the hetaira of ancient Greece or the Japanese geisha, were desirable not only for their beauty and sexual skills, but for the pleasure of their company and the status they conferred on the men who paid for their services. The most prized courtesans were accomplished musicians, learned and witty conversationalists, and gallant hostesses. These forerunners of the "bold and impudent" beauties who, with their outrageous dress, would defy the Magistrates of Pomp in the early eighteenth century, were the pride of Venice, celebrated throughout Europe.

While prostitution was accepted, Venetian society was less lenient toward women suspected of being witches—but more so than many of its neighbors. For a morning, these wretches were locked in the stocks and subjected to the taunts of their neighbors—though the condemned often gave as good as they got, adding to the popular spectacle. So hilarious were the proceedings that the Inquisition was cautious about using this form of punishment, which rarely seems to have had the deterrent effect the Holy Office sought. (Witchcraft was not prosecuted seriously as heresy until 1484, and even then Venice tended to display relative tolerance, perhaps carried over from its early identity as an international port or inspired by the enlightened self-interest that has always served it well.)

Certainly, self-interest largely motivated the city's attitude toward its Jewish population, a relationship that was marked by ambivalence for much of its long, and continuing, history. Over the two hundred years preceding the establishment of the *ghetto*, the quarter to which the Venetian Jews were confined at night, the Republic's official policies wavered constantly between severely restrictive measures and relative liberalism, especially toward Jewish residents of the overseas territories. The Venetian government settled on an unofficial policy that allowed the right hand of law to ignore what the left hand of practice was doing. Nonetheless, compared with some of its neighbors, Venice's reputation for tolerance—despite edicts requiring Jews to wear yellow badges and forbidding them to own property—was such that the city attracted refugees from other nations, especially the Papal States.

The Scuola Levantina, the only free-standing synagogue in the crowded *ghetto*, was built by Jews of the eastern Mediterranian. Its design is attributed to one of Venice's great architects, Baldassare Longhena, creator of the Church of Santa Maria della Salute.

The Splendid Decline

There now began the almost imperceptible ebb of the Venetian Republic, paradoxically contemporaneous with its centuries of most lavish display. As most of the world underwent the upheavals of the sixteenth century, Venice, always an independent agent, now withdrew even more from the worldly stage. The shocking Sack of Rome temporarily halted the Renaissance in the Eternal City; many artists fled to Venice, where throughout the century they received commissions to build and decorate houses of worship, public buildings, and palazzi. These were the centuries of the Venetian school of painting, known for its brash use of color and confident characterization, founded by the spiritual heirs of Giorgione and the great Bellini dynasty.

Meanwhile, in the eastern Mediterranean, Sultan Selim II was attacking Cyprus, one of the last Venetian outposts in the region. In 1570, Turkish war atrocities on the island inspired a new alliance, the Holy League, this time rallying Pope Gregory XIII, the kingdom of Spain, the duchy of Savoy, and the Knights of Malta to the Venetian cause. With a stunning naval victory in the Battle of Lepanto in 1571, the Christian forces won the war and thirty years of peace, but Venice was ultimately unable to retain Cyprus.

The Republic still held Paros, the Ionian Islands, and Crete, a fertile island rich with olive trees, grapevines, cotton, and flax. Venetian traders continued to trade with the Muslim countries of the eastern Mediterranean, some of them venturing even farther east. Venice's sources of wealth, though severely reduced, were sturdy, its autonomy virtually absolute—in fact, the Republic was excommunicated again in 1606–07 for refusing to follow certain policies of the Counter-Reformation. The history of Venice had long been a seamless fusion of the religious, the civic, and the commercial. The new Baroque look of palazzi, public buildings and churches suited the self-assured grandeur of the sublime city.

Although the plague never again reached the fury it had attained in 1348, its violent recurrences contributed to the city's increasing weakness—and gave it two of its most magnificent churches. In 1577, after a fierce return of the plague subsided, the Venetian Senate gratefully voted funds to build the Chiesa del Redentore, the Church of the Redeemer, commissioning Palladio to erect the splendid ex-voto on Giudecca. A devastating visitation of the "pest" in the late 1620s had taken forty-seven thousand lives, half the city's population, by 1630, when the Senate again voted to erect a church. The result was one of the most concrete examples of the public personality of Venice: the Church of Santa Maria della Salute, the Virgin of Health.

As the social forms of Venetian life became more stylized, its theater became more formal. Baroque architecture had brought the monumentalization of power to Venice, and Venetian theater copied that ever-so-theatrical style with its own form of monumentality. The improvisatory, subversive wit of *commedia dell'arte* gave way to stagy neoclassical presentations. In 1642, *The Coronation of Poppaea*, the first known historical opera, debuted at the Teatro di Santi Giovanni e Paolo, with music by Claudio Monteverdi.

Two years later, the Ottomans successfully laid siege to Khaniá, on Crete. Some twenty-five years later Venice would lose the entire island, its last major commercial stronghold in the eastern Mediterranean. In 1684, Venetian fleet commander Francesco Morosini won a number of battles against the Ottoman Turks, taking back the Peloponnesus—first conquered by Venice almost five hundred years before—and Athens. Nevertheless, the end of Venice's colonial strength was not far off: in 1718, with the Treaty of Passarowitz, the great Venetian Stato di Mare (Sea State) would be reduced to nothing more than the Ionian Islands and the Adriatic.

The eighteenth was the century of more than intellectual and aesthetic pleasures: once famous for its quasi-official sinners, Venice was becoming notorious for decadent opulence, laissez-faire hedonism, and corruption. In his savage 1758 fable *Candide*, Voltaire created Count Pococurante (roughly, "Carelittle"), "a noble Venetian." The count, a man of exquisite refinement, is the image of the disillusioned, world-weary sensualist who, no longer taking pleasure in anything, has retired to his palazzo on the Brenta. So clear-eyed was the century that a stock figure of theater—and, to some extent, of daily aristocratic life—was the *cavalier servente*, the gentleman friend and sometimes lover who escorted a lady to public events because her husband was otherwise occupied—with his mistress, it was understood.

Though oligarchical, the Republic had traditionally spread its wealth widely among its people; employment in the golden centuries had been high, the economy bustling and healthy. Now, with less of a commercial middle class, social differences became more extreme. Carlo Goldoni's hugely popular plays attracted large audiences to tales of clever servants outwitting foolish masters, themes harking back to ancient Roman times. Antonio Vivaldi, a violinist, ordained priest, and brilliant musical innovator, composed more than seven hundred works. His most famous composition, *The Four Seasons*, seems almost eerily to describe the history of La Serenissima, including, in the "Autumn" and "Winter" sections, a chill premonition of the end of a way of life.

Europe's wars of succession were being fought on Venetian territory, but without involving the Republic itself; and, though Venice went to sea twice more in the late eighteenth century, against the Barbary pirates, the city was increasingly sinking into its own myth. Where once Venice's aristocratic regime had coexisted with a generalized and active prosperity, now its system of government, without its commercial underpinnings, was ossified and without direction. Under the aegis of the revolution, Napoleon Bonaparte had all the pretext he needed to take over the Veneto when a local rebellion flared up against his presence during the wars with Austria. In May 1797, the last Venetian doge, Lodovico Manin, left the Palazzo Ducale.

Napoleon's secular regime closed some of the ancient churches and converted the great monastery complexes of the thirteenth and fourteenth centuries; the Church's treasures went to the conqueror. Public parks, one of the emblems of democracy, began to dot the city. It was the modern age: the French and Austrian occupiers not only continued La Serenissima's upkeep of the lagoon, but made improvements,

The sober and majestic Church of Santa Maria della Salute was raised by the Venetian Senate in fulfillment of a vow, when a virulent wave of the plague abated in 1630. The Virgin on top of the cupola's lantern is dressed as a capitana. The architect, Baldassare Longhena, one of Venice's greatest, designed the church to look like a crown, but did not live to see the glorious realization of his dream.

Like a ghost ship out of the past, a three-master moors within sight of the Arsenale, where once the great merchant and warships
sailed forth to make Venice the mightiest city of the Mediterranean.

such as opening a new port, revamping the Arsenale, and bringing in the railroad.

The eighteenth century had formalized the Grand Tour, part of every young European and American gentleman's education, and soon part of every well-brought-up young lady's finishing as well. With the advent of the ocean liner, transatlantic travel was commonplace among the privileged classes in the second half of the nineteenth century. Where Rome and Florence were de rigueur for cultural polish, Venice was a must for society, shopping, and leisure.

As seaside holidays became fashionable, Italians and others built vacation villas on the Lido, and entrepreneurs raised luxury oceanfront hotels like the Excelsior, built from 1898 to 1908 and today splendidly refurbished. The "playground of Europe" flourished, too, on a reputation for the good-humored sensuality that northern Europeans tended to attribute to the Italians generally. Venetian aristocrats, still attached to a way of life that was often now without economic roots, found it advantageous to rent or sell their palazzi to the flush newcomers.

It would be poetic, but utterly inaccurate, to describe nineteenth-century Venice as subsiding graciously into an eternal past, gently haunted by mannerly, satin-clad ghosts and elegant hedonists. In 1848, a popular uprising against the Austrian occupation brought the freedom fighter Daniele Manin out of prison and to the head of a heroic struggle. Under his leadership, the Venetians forced the Austrian forces to flee, albeit temporarily, and declared a new Republic—this one more in the contemporary vein. For fifteen months, they bravely survived military attacks, but

finally succumbed to hunger and cholera. The Austrians returned, only to lose the city for good in 1866, when Venice was integrated into united Italy.

Venice's location has always proved crucial to its history, and the twentieth century was no exception. The city occupied an important military position during World War I, which brought little physical damage, but many deaths among the civilian population. During the German occupation in the last years of World War II, the Resistance was active, and many Venetians sheltered their Jewish neighbors; nevertheless, some two hundred residents of the city died in the camps. Today, Venice dissents from the widespread right-wing politics of northern Italy. Perhaps the city's intimate geography nurtures its humanism: there is no escaping your neighbors, life is lived in public. For this reason, Venice is one of the world's safest cities: there is nowhere for perpetrators to hide.

For a thousand years, there has existed a myth of Venice— as distinct and complex as the scent of the sea and upheld most fervently by the Venetians themselves—proclaiming La Serenissima to be, in some way, history's chosen city. This assurance has nurtured the Republic's unique independence and strength—and perhaps serenity—and it continues to manifest itself in the city's refusal to give in to what once appeared to be an irresistible decline. The great trading days have come and gone, but the inner nature of Venice's mystical fascination remains in its genius for transformation: from sand to glass, stone to weightless artifice, thread to lace, paint and canvas to color, light, and mystery, and, most of all, daily life to timeless festival.

PART 2
VISTE

❧

PAGES 32–33: **Just around the bend, the Canal Grande enters the Basin of San Marco. On either side of the canal, the elegant *palazzi* recall the great families of Venice: Palazzo Corner, detto Cà Grande, Palazzo Venièr dei Leoni, Palazzo Tiepolo.**

ABOVE: **Napoleon called Piazza San Marco the drawing room of Europe, not only because of its aristocratic elegance and vast proportions, but because society's best and brightest crossed paths in its cafés.**

RIGHT: **Since time immemorial, the sea has fed Venice.**

꧁ꕥ꧂

ABOVE: **This imposing facade of the Palazzo Ducale faces into the courtyard; the ancient Roman statues were solemn reminders of civic duty. Above the seventeenth-century clock face is the doge Marino Grimani's coat of arms, surmounted by the *biretta*, or doge's hat.**

OPPOSITE: **Gold and blue are the colors of San Marco. The lunette's mosaic represents the Ascension; its celestial splendor is crowned by a band of sculptures led by Saint Michael Archangel.**

PAGES 38–39: **From high above piazza San Marco, looking north to the great meander of the Canal Grande, Venice looks like many other Italian cities. Yet winding among its houses and calli, the rii carry the timeless tides in ancient rhythm.**

ABOVE: **The Loggia Foscara, also called the Loggia of Justice, in the Doges' Palace, overlooks the Piazzetta, where punishment was meted out. It was in this loggia, too, that the celebrations surrounding the coronation of the doges' wives were held, as well as the guilds' exhibitions.**

ABOVE: **An ornate nineteenth-century wrought-iron lamppost pays homage to the grandeur of the spires and cupolas of Saint Mark's Basilica.**

❦

LEFT: **Frozen in time, a boat dreams in the warm rays of the Venetian sun.**

ABOVE: **All that remains of the ostentation of the Golden Age gondolas of Venice is the rhythmical decoration of the beak. The horizontal elements are traditional, their origin lost in the ages.**

❧

Campo Santo Stefano in the sestiere San Marco is one of Venice's largest and one of the Venetians' favorites. La Serenissima has its own unique names for city sites: the word *campo*—"field"—recalls the long-ago mainland days of the Republic; smaller spaces are *campielli*; and streets are *calli orcallette*. The Renaissance Palazzo Loredan, above, is one of the square's jewels.

OPPOSITE: **The country palazzi by Palladio and others are the aristocratic traces of the Stato di Terra, the Venetian Republic's possessions on land. Many of these are still lived in—at least part of the year—by descendants of those who built them. Venice is, not surprisingly, one of the world capitals of restoration.**

ABOVE: **Faded but beloved, a humble fresco of the Virgin and Child is sheltered by an architectural flourish, and honored by a length of opulent brocade.**

⋰✦⋱

ABOVE: **In an ancient gesture, a Venetian repairs his nets, the tools of his trade. Although tourism is the city's premier industry, life behind the scenes is much like that of any Italian seaport.**

RIGHT: **Palladio's Villa Corner, its façade reworked in later centuries, is one of several palazzi built by the powerful Venetian dynasty that gave the Republic four doges and a queen of Cyprus.**

OPPOSITE: **On the north side of Piazza San Marco rises the Clock Tower, built in the last years of the fifteenth century. The clock face, whose color scheme of blue and gold echoes that of the nearby Basilica, tells the date, hour, phases of the moon, and position of the sun in the zodiac.**

ABOVE: **This proud winged lion, timeless emblem of La Serenissima and a masterpiece of the sculptor's art, displays an ageless wisdom.**

LEFT: In the misty distance, the island of San Giorgio Maggiore, home of a church and monastery designed by the celebrated Andrea Palladio, displays its unmistakable silhouette. The Benedictine monastery numbers only a few members of the order, but in its heyday the monks received exalted guests such as Cosimo de' Medici.

ABOVE: Across the Canale San Marco from the Palazzo Ducale, on the island of San Giorgio Maggiore, the campanile erected in 1791 is a tribute to the bell tower of Piazza San Marco and is surmounted by a statue of the soldier-saint George. The 190-foot (60m) tower offers the most all-embracing panorama of Venice, one of the most beautiful views in Italy.

Any minute now, a gondola from centuries past could pull up and moor at the traditional red-striped posts
across a *rio* from a restaurant.

A long-established bakery in Burano provides the neighborhood's daily bread, *merenda*—the after-school snack—
or a plate of pastry to celebrate a special occasion.

LEFT: Beyond the hundred isles of Venice, Burano, once a fishing community, still preserves its working-class identity. Where La Serenissima's waterfront palazzi boast magnificent architecture, the more humble homes of Burano are known for their bright array of colors.

ABOVE: In the peaceful *calli* of Burano, old age has its pleasures—the heart-filling warmth of the sun, and the bright beauty of simple things.

❧

OPPOSITE: Just as the *campi* recall the fields of terra firma, so the *rii* hark back to the rivers of the mainland. A Renaissance façade fronts on the narrow waterway, its *porta d'acqua* still ready to receive guests.

ABOVE: The two-tiered Bridge of Sighs led from the grim prisons of the Palazzo Ducale to the cells of the Palazzo dei Prigioni. The most famous person known to have crossed the fateful bridge was Casanova—who claimed to have escaped the Piombi, the hellish attics beneath the lead roofs of the Doges' Palace.

PAGES 60–61: **The Doges' Palace is one of the world's wonders, a confection wedding the greatness of Venice and the genius of Italy's greatest artists, whose masterpieces can be seen in the locations for which they were made. At the same time, it unites the unparalleled magnificence of the Republic's Golden Age and its down-to-earth politics: on the canal side, within the ground-floor loggia, is the Gate of Grain.**

ABOVE: **Left to right, Gothic to Renaissance, the rhythm of the façades of the palazzi reflects the passage of time. And always, the intimate relationship to water.**

The grand courtyard of the Ducal Palace is practically a piazza in itself, a Renaissance tour-de-force combining opulence and restraint.

The Scala dei Giganti, or Giants' Stairway, shown here, leads to the landing where the new doges were crowned.

ABOVE: **Time and tide, decay defied by bravado and brilliant color: Venice is eternal, the ages etched in every aspect of the landscape.**

RIGHT: **The Basilica di San Marco represents a medieval miracle of construction, decoration—and opulent pride. Part of its grandeur arises from the monumental simplicity of its Greek-cross floor plan, while the sequence of arches and cupolas, all sheathed in gold mosaic, bespeak both the splendors of heaven and the greatness of the Republic.**

As they have for centuries, the sculptures of Christ and the Prophets

greet those entering the Basilica of San Marco.

In the thirteenth century, as Venice's commercial empire was expanding, so, too, were the city's public spaces.
The square in front of San Marco was widened, and to respect the proportions (and importance) of the church,
it was decided to increase the height of the cupolas with lanterns—that also let light into the
gilded interiors—surmounted by onion domes.

❧

ABOVE: **A sunlit window exudes peace in the neighborhood of the Ponte Novo, or New Bridge, in the quarter where Armenian merchants once lived and traded.**

RIGHT: **Daily life goes on as it does the world over, as it did during the days when Venice was La Dominante, on land as on sea.**

Two armed and winged figures reflect Venice's dual identity, as a city of war and treaties, and as a locus of passion.

Life goes on as usual, even during the *acqua alte*, or high waters, the periodic flooding that at times
has threatened Venice's treasures and the city's very foundations.

❧

ABOVE: **Since 1720, Café Florian, in Piazza San Marco, has welcomed the intelligentsia of Europe and beyond.**
At Carnival time, the café admits only those whose costumes they deem worthy.

OPPOSITE: **Known as Venice's living room, the Piazza San Marco is one of the most stunning public squares in the world.**
Here, staff ready the tables at one the the piazza's open-air cafés.

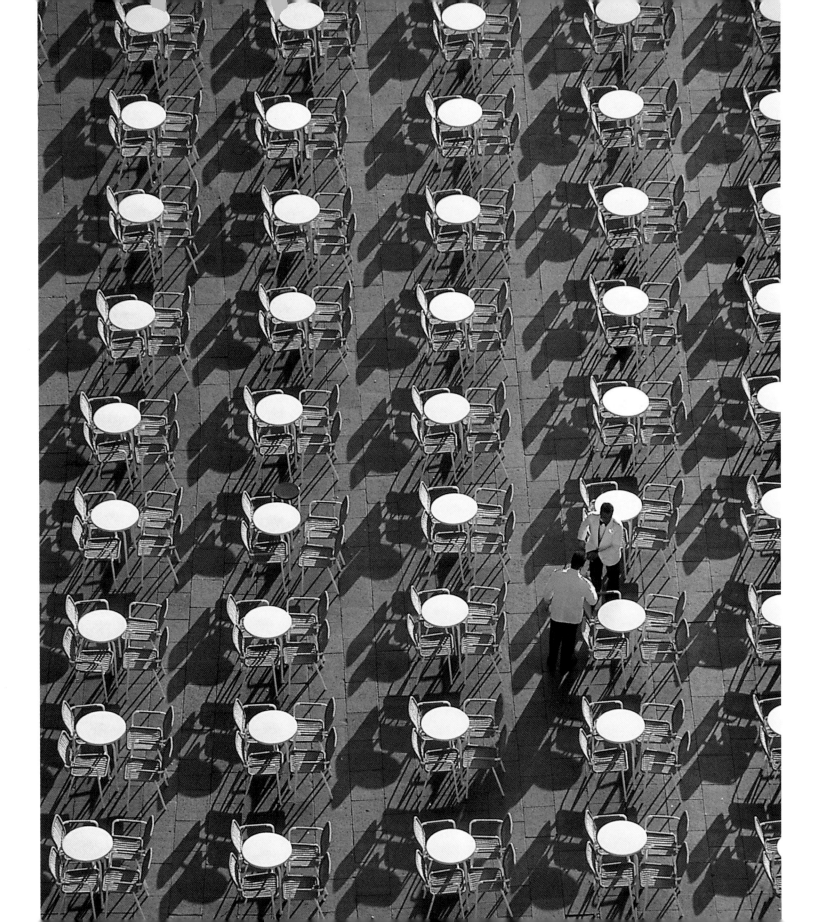

OPPOSITE: **All conversation seems brilliant in a resplendent environment such as Florian's, whose Enlightenment decor displays touches of Napoleon's imperial nineteenth century.**

ABOVE: **Arabesques and eight-pointed stars borrowed from Islamic design recall the long centuries of Venice's relations with the Ottoman Empire.**

Its buildings reincarnated time and again over one thousand years, San Giorgio Maggiore slumbers beneath the snow, just as the gondolas dip and rise with the lagoon's gentle tides, dreaming of summer visitors.

ABOVE: The most Venetian of churches—after
San Marco—is the one the locals affectionately
call San Zanipolo. Here, one of the three
noble naves proudly exhibits its seemingly
weightless thirteenth-century ogival arches.

RIGHT: La Fenice, one of Italy's most beloved opera
houses, has risen more than once to receive the
world's greatest performers—and
most glittering audiences.

꧁

ABOVE: Ghostly frescoed courtiers climb the grand staircase of
Villa Giustinian, built in Murano in 1689 by a bishop of that name
who moved his see from Torcello.

RIGHT: This spiral staircase rising to a skylight in the ceiling brings
its sweeping nature-inspired lines to the Villa Corner, renovated in the
nineteenth century, and still one of the jewels of the Brenta River.

LEFT: **Saint Erasmus is Venice's cornucopia, rich in vineyards and gardens. The farmers of Saint Erasmus produce the legendary delicacies and the fragrant mainstays of Venetian cuisine. Carefully packed, like the precious commodities they are, the luscious seasonal vegetables and fruit will arrive at the Rialto markets still touched with dawn's dew.**

ABOVE: **This market stand, amid the bustle of the Rialto, displays the best fruits and vegetables from near and far—just as its forebears did a thousand years ago. Venice is, after all, an Italian city at heart, where daily life is lived at a human pace, with time and appreciation for the good things.**

The ancient islands of the lagoon, sheltered by the long barrier of the Lido, are as far from the epochal grandeur of the *sestieri* as they are from the Lido's sophisticated leisure.

Though boat traffic on the *rii* is not what it was during the great days of La Serenissima, the tiny canals that
thread through Venice are useful in other ways.

In Venice, as elsewhere, good fences make good neighbors.

The Republic's tradition of well-secured diplomacy lives on.

This playful *putto* may have adorned an eighteenth-century staircase, or witnessed forbidden flirtations in an aristocratic park. His mischievous air seems unfazed, as he waits to see what the next chapter of his life will bring.

The treasures of dismantled palazzi and Carnivals past pour in gilded, extravagant profusion—and sometimes
exuberant bad taste—from one of Venice's many antique shops.

ABOVE: **Hidden on a quiet backstreet, a tavern-turned-hotel beckons passersby to stop in for an evening of fine wine and revelry.**

OPPOSITE: **The Fortuny Museum, housed in a fifteenth-century palazzo, displays the collection of the twentieth-century painter and set designer Mariano Fortuny y Madrazo.**

OPPOSITE: **Carnival in Venice, revived in recent decades, offers a chance to experience another existence in the city of innumerable lives.**

ABOVE: **La Serenissima's artisans were the source of the legendary wealth that poured into the city. Their skills, like a mysterious alchemy, transformed the mundane into the miraculous.**

PAGE 96: **Despite the dazzled millions who arrive from the mainland, the sea will never cease to be Venice's mystical destiny.**

INDEX

PHOTO CREDITS